ariana grande

truly yours

ariana grande

truly yours

by emily klein

SCHOLASTIC INC.

Front cover: Tonya Wise/Invision/AP Images; cover background: 9comeback/Shutterstock; back cover, top to bottom: Alberto E. Rodriguez/WireImage/Getty Images; Charley Gallay/Getty Images; Uri Schanker/FilmMagic/Getty Images; Kevin Winter/WireImage/Getty Images; p3: Dan MacMedan/ WireImage/Getty Images; p6: Samuel-Christophe Tedjasukmana/PatrickMcMullan.com/Sipa USA/ AP Images; p8: Jim Spellman/Getty Images; p11: Walter McBride/Corbis Images; p13: Sbukley/ Dreamstime; p14: Jeffrey Mayer/WireImage/Getty Images; p16: Larry Busacca/Getty Images; p17: Noel Vasquez/Getty Images; p18: kathclick/Bigstock; p21: Lisa Rose/Nickelodeon/AP Images; p22: Evan Agostini/Invision/AP Images; p24: John Shearer/Invision for MTV/AP Images; p27: Charles Sykes/AP Images; p28: John Shearer/Invision/AP Images; p31: John Shearer/Invision/AP Images; p32: Charles Sykes/Invision/AP Images; p35: Photo Works/Bigstock; 36: Jeff Kravitz/FilmMagic/Getty Images; p37: Johnny Nunez/WireImage/Getty Images; p39: Rex Features/AP Images; p40: Ben Hider/Invision/AP Images; p43: Gregg DeGuire/WireImage/Getty Images; p44: Lance Murphey/Getty Images; p46: Charles Sykes/Invision/AP Images.

UNAUTHORIZED:
This book is not sponsored by or affiliated with Ariana Grande or anyone involved with her.

Copyright © 2014 by Scholastic
ISBN 978-0-545-72285-8

Published by Scholastic Inc.
SCHOLASTIC and associated logos are trademarks and/or registered trademarks of Scholastic Inc.

10 9 8 7 6 5 4 3 2 1   14 15 16 17 18 19/0

Printed in the U.S.A.   40
First printing, September 2014

table of contents

introduction

Have you ever imagined living the life of a pop superstar? How about being compared to singer Mariah Carey? Or getting standing ovations from celebrities like Lady Gaga? Well, Ariana Grande has lived all of these amazing experiences and more.

She got her big break on the hit television show *Victorious*. Her character was so adored that Nickelodeon gave her a costarring role in its spin-off series, *Sam & Cat*. Sounds like an awesome life, right? Well, Ariana's world hasn't always been red carpets and music tours. She worked hard to reach the top. Yet even with all her success, she's still not done climbing.

CHAPTER 1

growing up

Ariana Grande-Butera enjoyed a sunny childhood in beautiful Boca Raton, Florida. She was born on June 26, 1993, to parents Joan Grande and Edward Butera. Ariana has many happy memories from her younger years.

She loved going to the beach and watching Nickelodeon. She also remembers good times at her family's annual Christmas party and family reunions. "I had a really great childhood and I loved growing up in Boca," she told fans during a live chat session on the fan site ArianaGrande.org.

Ariana has always been super-close with her fam. She told fans during that same live chat session that she considers her grandparents to be "the greatest people on earth." Ariana also shares a special bond with her half brother, Frankie Grande, and her mom. She told *Neon Limelight*, "Since I was a little girl, my mom would make me feel like I was a little star."

Ariana decided she wanted to be a performer when she was still very young. She would watch shows like *All That* and *The Amanda Show* and think, "I want to do that," she told the *Sun Sentinel*. She said in the same interview, "When I was four, I called 411, and asked to speak to Nick Studios. . . . I told a receptionist I wanted to be on *All That*. She said I needed an agent."

When Ariana was eight years old, she got a surprising nudge to follow her dream. She was singing karaoke on a cruise ship and Gloria Estefan was there! Gloria told Ariana that she should keep performing because that's what she was meant to do. Ariana took this advice seriously. She performed for children's theaters and community theaters. And she also did stand-up comedy routines for her grandparents almost every day. All of her practice eventually paid off.

When Ariana was fifteen years old, she got her big break on Broadway. She landed the role of Charlotte in the musical *13*. "It all happened so quickly," she told the *Sun*

Sentinel. Even though Ariana loved working, jumping to Broadway right from middle school was hard. She told *Neon Limelight,* "I was like, yay, no more school!" But then she realized she would spend every day dancing for more than twelve hours. Ariana did not back down from the hard work, though. She shined in her new role.

And while her star was rising in New York City, it didn't take long for Hollywood to notice. Ariana's childhood dream was about to come true!

Victorious

Ariana started the audition process for *Victorious*—a Nickelodeon show about teens at a performing arts high school—while she was still in New York performing in *13*. She told the *Sun Sentinel*, "The original audition was [where] everybody had the same character, boy or girl, and you had to read the lines and act a little crazy. They called me back and asked me to try for Cat." Ariana flew to Los Angeles for her callback. Then she had a few screen tests. Finally, she got a call from the show's creator. Ariana had won the role! "I almost died," she told MissOandFriends.com. Ariana and her mom packed their bags and moved to Los Angeles.

Victorious premiered on March 27, 2010. Ariana sparkled on-screen, but she looked different. She played Cat with bright red hair! "That was Dan Schneider's [the creator's] vision for my character. It was totally genius and I can't see my character any other way," she told the *Sun Sentinel*. Ariana also told *Seventeen* magazine, "I get to be myself when I have brown hair and then I get to be Cat when I have red hair!" Fans loved Ariana and the show. *Victorious* won "Favorite TV Show" at the Kid's Choice Awards in 2012 and 2013.

Then Nickelodeon stunned fans by announcing that *Victorious*'s third season would be its last. Even the show's star, Victoria Justice, was shocked. Dan Schneider explained to heartbroken fans that most Nickelodeon live-action shows only run for about sixty episodes—which was almost the number of episodes *Victorious* had filmed. Luckily, Ariana's character had been chosen for an exciting new spin-off series. Ariana's fans could still watch her on TV!

lucky cat

After *Victorious* ended, Nickelodeon decided to feature Ariana's *Victorious* character, Cat, and *iCarly*'s character, Sam, in a buddy comedy called *Sam & Cat*. The show is about two unlikely besties who start a babysitting service together. Sam is played by one of Ariana's offscreen buds, Jennette McCurdy. (The two stars also share the same birthday, but a year apart.) Ariana told *Seventeen,* "I am so lucky to be working with Jennette McCurdy. . . . I used to watch *iCarly* and think, 'Wow, Jennette is . . . so good.'"

Over four million people tuned in to watch the *Sam & Cat* premiere on June 8, 2013. That first show was Nickelodeon's biggest live-action debut in three years. It also topped the iTunes TV episode chart. *Sam & Cat* was a hit!

Fans got to enjoy Ariana in other acting projects as well. She guest starred on *iCarly*, had a role in the original TV movie *Swindle*, and was the voice of Princess Diaspro in the animated series *Winx Club*. And in 2012, she starred as Snow White in the Pasadena Playhouse show *A Snow White Christmas*.

But even though Ariana has had an amazing acting career, she still feels most comfortable singing. As she explained to *LA Stage Times*, "I was literally born with it. It's like my purpose." Launching a singing career was a natural next step for this talented TV star.

4

ariana on the mic

Singing has always been Ariana's first passion. In 2011, while she was still on *Victorious*, Ariana signed with Universal Republic Records. She was lucky enough to collaborate with some serious musical

A-listers on her first album. Ariana shared the mic with Big Sean, Mika, Nathan Sykes (from The Wanted), and Mac Miller. She told RollingStone.com, "Everybody on the record is a very close friend of mine. . . . I recorded him [Mac Miller] rapping, while I was simultaneously baking cookies for him."

Even though making the album was lots of fun, it was still hard work. It took three years to complete. Ariana explained to *Glamour,* "By the end of the writing process, I had to completely rerecord the songs that we had written in the beginning because my voice had changed so much."

Once the album was done, Ariana had to decide on its title. She originally liked *Daydreamin'* but then changed her mind. She explained in a *Myspace* interview that she sent a mass text to her besties asking them for help. One friend suggested she "sign it like a

love letter" because the album is so personal. Ariana immediately texted back, "Oh my God, *Yours Truly*. What about that?" Everyone loved the idea, and the name stuck.

As for the album's sound, she told *Billboard* that it's "throwback R&B, soulful, but poppy." Ariana's breakout single, "The Way," featuring Mac Miller, debuted on *On Air with Ryan Seacrest* in March 2013. It instantly lit up the charts. "The Way" flew to number 10 on the Billboard Hot 100 and sold 219,000 downloads in its first week. "Baby I" was the next song released, followed by "Right Here."

While Ariana's fans were rocking to her music on the radio, she was busy rehearsing for live performances. In August, Ariana headed out on her *Listening Sessions* tour. As she explained in a GRAMMY.com interview: "The Listening Sessions tour is about introducing my fans to the album in a very intimate way. . . . We're playing more intimate venues and performing the entire album top to bottom."

The tour created a huge spark. When *Yours Truly* was finally released in early September 2013, it hit the charts at number one. Ariana told *Billboard*, "I can't even express how happy I am, how grateful I am, to be taken seriously as an artist." Ariana was so excited that she strained her vocal cords celebrating at a party for the album. She reassured her fans in a video on Instagram, though, telling them: "I just lost my voice . . . but I'm completely fine."

Even though Ariana already had many musical successes to celebrate at this point in her career, her breakout performance was yet to come.

a standout performance

On November 24, 2013, Ariana stepped onto the stage at the American Music Awards in a long, fitted, red-sequined dress. Her hair was fashioned in her signature half-up/half-down style. With only four backup singers accompanying her, Ariana belted out a short, a cappella version of "The Way," followed by her song "Tattooed Heart." Her vocals were flawless. The star-studded crowd went wild! Even Lady Gaga gave her a standing ovation.

Old and new fans took to Twitter to sing Ariana's praises. Kelly Clarkson even chimed in, tweeting, "Saw a clip of @ArianaGrande singing on the AMA's. That's how it's done ladies and gentlemen."

Ariana's night wasn't over, though. Later in the show, she won the New Artist of the Year award. She beat out Macklemore & Ryan Lewis, Phillip Phillips, Imagine Dragons, and Florida Georgia Line. "Oh my God, I'm so nervous! Thank you so much," she stammered to the audience. "I have the most loving, supportive fans in the world. I'm so nervous." She continued, "My mom made me this thing, and I have it in here so that I don't forget anybody," as she pulled out a list of people to thank.

After that evening, everyone knew Ariana Grande's name. She was a superstar! People even started comparing her to the singer Mariah Carey. She told *Complex* magazine, "It's a massive compliment."

CHAPTER

6

arianators

It's obvious that Ariana has a special relationship with her fans, who are called Arianators. On her Twitter page she says, "My fans are family." And she told *Complex* magazine, "I've always had an open, honest relationship with my fans."

Ariana often posts the happenings in her life as they occur. When she signed with Republic Records, she immediately tweeted the exciting news along with a picture of herself holding the contract.

She also credits her fans with her success. "As soon as 'The Way' came out, it sort of climbed the iTunes chart because of my fans," she said in a GRAMMY.com interview. "And it was amazing that they got it to number one."

When asked to describe her fans in three words, Ariana told *Billboard* they are "dedicated, amazing, and unbreakable." One time she tweeted to Arianators: "I tear up just looking at your tweets recently, so I need to express my gratitude—I'm the happiest I've ever been . . ."

Ariana also sees herself as a role model to her fans. She told *M* magazine, "I consider myself to be their big sister."

With her massive fan base, Klout.com named Ariana one of the five most influential actresses on social media. Ariana told *Billboard*, "I can't really go anywhere without being stopped for a photo anymore, but now it's not just little kids." Fans swarmed the star during a brief trip to Paris in November 2013. Ariana feeds her fan frenzy with live chats where she'll answer fans' questions. She also offers "follow sprees" on Twitter. During these times, she will "follow" any Arianator who asks—or as many as Twitter will allow.

Ariana has lots of famous fans, too. "I love her voice," R&B singer-songwriter and producer Kenneth "Babyface" Edmonds told *Complex* magazine. Katy Perry told Sirius XM listeners, "I think she has the best female vocal in pop music today . . . And she's the sweetest girl and I just wish her the best."

Demi Lovato also thinks she's awesome. "She has vocals that are just unbelievable, and I have so much respect for her because she is a true singer. . . . I think she's going to be a huge name. . . ."

ariana unscripted

Ariana is always super busy with work. She told the *Guardian,* "When I was making the album, I would start [filming] *Sam & Cat* at 6:30 in the morning and finish at 8:30 [p.m.], then go to the studio till midnight and get home at 1 a.m." She was so driven, not even illness stopped her. She told her fans on Twitter that she recorded "Tattooed Heart" and "Honeymoon Avenue" when she was very sick.

At one point, Ariana felt overwhelmed by everything she had on her plate. Then she got some awesome advice from another celeb. Ariana told *Billboard* that Michelle Williams

from Destiny's Child told her, "You need to make time every day to have twenty minutes of quiet time . . .You need to eat, you need to sleep, you need to rest, and you need to be happy and enjoy it."

When Ariana isn't working she likes to tweet and Instagram. She also enjoys listening to music—mostly soul, R&B, and pop. And she loves spending time with her three adorable dogs: Ophelia, Toulouse, and Coco. (Fans can even follow her dogs on their own Instagram account!) When she has time, Ariana watches *America's Next Top Model* and *Project Runway*. She also loves *The Lord of the Rings*, Harry Potter, scary movies, dinosaurs, science, and aliens.

Ariana is also into eating healthy. She told *Complex* magazine, "I only eat salmon, vegetables, and fruits—super healthy." Ariana recently went a step further and became vegan. That means she does not eat any animal products. She only consumes grains, beans, legumes, fruits, and veggies. She tweeted, "I've eaten organically since I was little and always kept meat minimal but today marks my first day as a 100% Vegan!!!! Joyous day." She even has an organic garden in her backyard.

As for style, Ariana has her very own signature look. She told *Glamour*, "I tend to keep it very classic. I like very girly, retro-inspired, feminine floral things. I'm not very edgy." Ariana often wears a pretty skirt with a blouse or halter, and fabulous heels. She buys most of her clothes at LF, Urban Outfitters, and stores on Melrose Avenue and Rodeo Drive in Los Angeles. Her favorite clothing designer is Chanel, and her favorite shoe designer is Yves Saint Laurent.

Ariana also takes a stand on issues

she feels passionate about. She wrote a heartfelt blog post against bullying for the *Huffington Post*. And she co-founded Kids Who Care, which is a singing group that performs for charities. She has also taught music and dance lessons to kids in Gugulethu, South Africa, through the organization Broadway in South Africa.

So, what's next for this glittering star? Ariana has finished recording her second album, and her single, "Problem," sold more than 400,000 digital copies in its first week of sales in May, 2014.

And she told *Glamour*, "I love making music and performing for my fans, and I want to be happy and doing what I love . . . if I'm lucky I'll be able to keep doing this. I love it. I'm very happy."

just the facts

full name: Ariana Grande-Butera

hometown: Boca Raton, Florida

parents' names: Joan Grande and Edward Butera

sibling: Frankie Grande

pets: dogs Ophelia, Toulouse, and Coco

height: 5' 0"

music icons: India.Arie, Imogen Heap, Frank Ocean, Whitney Houston, and Judy Garland

would most like to sing with: Frank Sinatra

go-to karaoke song: "Lady Marmalade"

favorite disney princess: Aurora (Sleeping Beauty)

guilty pleasure: dark chocolate (even though she is allergic)

favorite restaurant in los angeles: Toast

all-time idol: Marilyn Monroe

favorite childhood movie: *The Wizard of Oz*

first song she ever sang: "Somewhere Over the Rainbow"

nickname: Ari

website: arianagrande.com

twitter: twitter.com/ArianaGrande

instagram: instagram.com/arianagrande